Unleashing Your Inner Power: Mastering Your Mindset for Personal Transformation

About The Author

The author of this book hails from the vibrant continent of Africa, born in Muwah Village within the Pinyin Clan. Known as HRM Muluh Taka, he embodies the essence of a traditional leader deeply committed to the welfare of those he serves.

His academic journey includes a master's degree in Business Administration from MANCOSA and a master's degree in Management in Innovation Studies from the University of Witwatersrand, reflecting his profound belief in the transformative power of education.

Drawing from his extensive experience in empowering individuals and communities, he passionately shares his insights in this book, believing fervently that through reading and application, individuals can unlock their innate potential.

As a recognized authority in fostering personal and collective growth, HRM Muluh Taka adeptly guides readers on a journey of self-discovery and empowerment in "Unleashing Your Inner Power."

Why Did I Write This Book

In a world brimming with untapped potential, where individuals yearn to break free from the shackles of self- doubt and societal constraints, "Unleashing Your Inner Power" emerges as a beacon of empowerment. This book transcends mere words; it serves as a transformative manifesto, a roadmap to unlocking one's fullest potential. But what motivated HRM Muluh Taka to pen this profound guide? What inspired him to distill his wisdom and experiences into these pages? The answers lie in his unwavering commitment to uplifting individuals and communities, and his steadfast belief in the boundless power that resides within each of us.

HRM Muluh Taka's journey toward writing "Unleashing Your Inner Power" was shaped by his upbringing in Muwah Village and his lineage within the esteemed Clan. Immersed in an environment rich with tradition and community spirit, he bore witness to the profound impact of collective empowerment. These formative experiences ignited a passion within him, a burning desire to empower others, to serve as a guide on their journey to unlocking their innate potential.

Beyond his academic achievements, HRM Muluh Taka draws from a wealth of lived experiences in empowering individuals and communities. As a traditional leader deeply invested in the welfare of his people, he has firsthand witnessed the transformative effects of empowerment initiatives.

Through both trials and triumphs, he has honed his understanding of human potential, and it is this profound wisdom that he generously shares with readers. "Unleashing Your Inner Power" transcends its status as a mere book; it serves as a call to action, an invitation to embark on a journey of self-discovery and empowerment.

HRM Muluh Taka's words resonate with authenticity and empathy, guiding readers toward harnessing their inner strength and realizing their aspirations. Whether one seeks personal fulfillment, professional success, or societal change, this book offers invaluable insights and practical guidance to unlock one's fullest potential.

Through his words, HRM Muluh Taka inspires readers to embrace their inherent greatness, to believe in the power of their dreams, and to embark on a journey of self-discovery and transformation. As readers engage with the pages of this book, may they find the courage to unleash their inner power and forge a brighter, more empowered future for themselves and those around them.

Copyright

This book is not a work of fiction. Names, characters, places, and incidents are the product of the author's experiences.The views expressed in this book are those of the author and do not necessarily represent the views of any organization or entity associated with the author.

While the author has made every effort to provide accurate and up-to-date information, the contents of this book are for informational purposes only. They should not be considered professional or expert advice to your unique circumstances. Readers are encouraged to consult relevant professionals for advice tailored to their circumstances.

The author and publisher assume no responsibility or liability for any errors or omissions in the content of this book. The information contained herein is provided on an "as- is" basis, with no guarantees of completeness, accuracy, or timeliness.

For additional information, please contact: muwahpalace@gmail.com

Thank you for respecting the intellectual property rights and the effort put forth in creating this book.

I appreciate your support.

My Promise to You

As you embark on the journey within the pages of "Unleashing Your Inner Power," I extend to you my heartfelt promise. Within these words, you will find not just guidance, but a steadfast commitment to your empowerment and growth.

I promise to share with you the insights gleaned from a lifetime of experiences, rooted in the rich soil of tradition and community spirit. Through my words, I pledge to illuminate the path toward unlocking your innate potential, offering practical tools and heartfelt encouragement every step of the way.

Together, we will navigate the landscapes of self-discovery and transformation, drawing upon the boundless reservoir of strength that resides within you.

With authenticity and empathy, I promise to stand by your side as you embrace your inherent greatness and chart a course toward a brighter, more empowered future.

Your journey begins here, and my promise to you is that you will not walk it alone and that you are set to win.

Preface

You are welcome to the transformative journey that lies ahead within the pages of "Unleashing Your Inner Power." As you hold this book in your hands, I invite you to embark on an exploration of self-discovery, empowerment, and boundless potential.

Within these chapters, you will discover not only words, but a guiding light, a beacon of hope and possibility. For me, the genesis of this book stems from a deep-rooted commitment to uplift individuals and communities, inspired by my upbringing in Muwah Village and my heritage within the Pinyin Clan.

From these foundational experiences emerged a fervent desire to empower others, to share the insights gained through a lifetime of learning and growth. Drawing from academic achievements and lived experiences alike, I offer you wisdom woven from the threads of civilization, tradition, resilience, and human connection. Through both triumphs and challenges, I have come to understand the profound truth that each of us possesses a reservoir of untapped potential and power waiting to be unleashed.

"Unleashing Your Inner Power" is more than just a book; it is a promise of transformation, of empowerment, of a brighter tomorrow. Within these pages, you will find the tools and encouragement to embark on your own journey of self-discovery, to embrace your inherent greatness, and to realize the dreams that stir within your soul.

So, dear reader, I invite you to turn the page and begin this adventure with an open heart and a steadfast determination. Together, let us unlock the door to possibility and step into a future filled with boundless potential. Your journey starts now.

Who Should Read This Book?

"Unleashing Your Inner Power" is a profound exploration into the depths of human potential and a guidebook for anyone who dares to dream, anyone who seeks to break free from the constraints of self-doubt, and anyone who yearns to forge a path toward personal empowerment and fulfillment. This book is for:

1. **Seekers of Self-Discovery:** If you find yourself on a quest for deeper self-understanding, if you long to unearth your true essence and purpose in life, then this book is for you. Through introspective exercises and insightful reflections, "Unleashing Your Inner Power" offers a roadmap to self-discovery, guiding you on a journey toward greater self-awareness and authenticity.

2. **Aspiring Leaders:** Whether you aspire to lead others or simply lead yourself toward your goals, this book holds invaluable lessons in leadership and empowerment. Drawing from the author's experiences as a traditional leader and academic achiever, "Unleashing Your Inner Power" equips you with the tools and mindset needed to inspire and influence those around you, fostering positive change in your personal and professional spheres.

3. **Individuals Seeking Personal Growth:** Are you ready to step out of your comfort zone and embrace growth and transformation? Whether you're facing challenges in your career, relationships, or personal development, this book offers practical guidance and motivational insights to help you overcome obstacles and reach new heights of success and fulfillment.

4. **Community Builders:** If you are passionate about making a positive impact in your community, "Unleashing Your Inner Power" provides inspiration and actionable strategies for fostering collective empowerment

and social change. Whether you're a community organizer, activist, or volunteer, the principles outlined in this book can help you harness the power of collaboration and collective action to create a brighter future for all.

5. **Anyone Ready to Embrace Their Potential:** Ultimately, "Unleashing Your Inner Power" is for anyone who dares to believe in themselves and their ability to create the life they desire. Whether you're a student, professional, entrepreneur, or retiree, this book serves as a reminder that within you lies a reservoir of untapped potential—a power waiting to be unleashed. So, if you're ready to embark on a journey of self- discovery, empowerment, and transformation, then this book is for you.

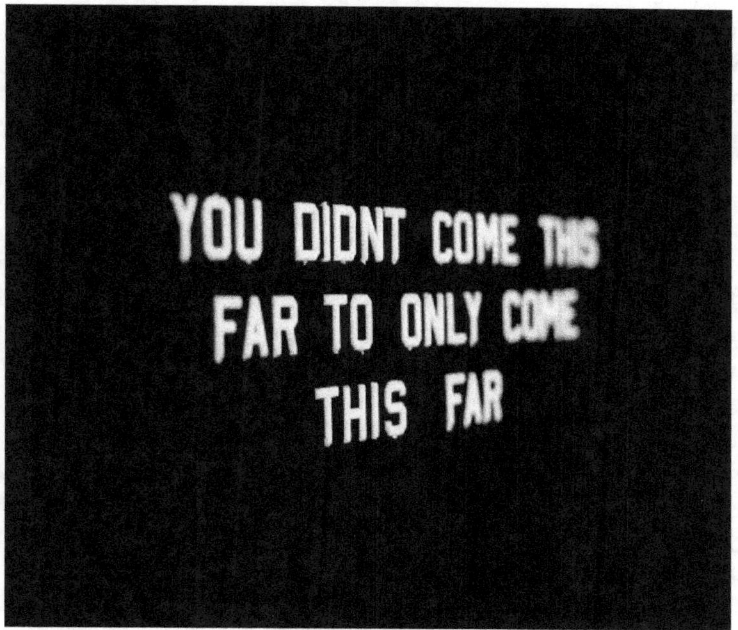

Acknowledgments

As I reflect on the journey of bringing "Unleashing Your Inner Power" to fruition, I am overwhelmed with gratitude for the countless individuals whose support and contributions have made this book possible. First and foremost, I extend my deepest appreciation to my family and loved ones, whose unwavering encouragement and belief in me have been the driving force behind this endeavor. Your love, patience, and understanding have sustained me through the challenges and triumphs of the writing process.

I am profoundly grateful to the Pinyin Clan and all its villages, whose rich heritage and collective spirit have shaped my worldview and inspired my commitment to empowerment. Your resilience, wisdom, and sense of unity continue to guide and inspire me every day.

To my mentors and teachers, both past and present, I offer my heartfelt thanks for imparting invaluable knowledge, wisdom, and guidance throughout my academic and personal journey. Your mentorship has been instrumental in shaping my understanding of leadership, empowerment, and the human experience.

I am indebted to the countless individuals who have shared their stories, insights, and experiences with me over the years. Your openness and willingness to engage in dialogue have enriched my understanding of human potential and fueled my passion for empowerment.

I extend my gratitude to the readers and supporters of "Unleashing Your Inner Power," whose enthusiasm and engagement have fueled my determination to share this message of empowerment with the world. Your feedback, encouragement, and support have been a source of inspiration and motivation throughout the writing process. Finally, to all those who have played a role, large or small, in bringing "Unleashing Your Inner Power" to fruition, I extend my heartfelt thanks. May this book serve as a beacon of hope, inspiration, and empowerment for all who dare to dream and strive for a brighter, more empowered future.

Table Of Contents

What do I want to accomplish?

What is important to me?

Chapter 1: Understanding the Power of Your Mindset

The Role of Mindset in Personal Transformation

In the journey of personal transformation, our mindset is one of the most crucial elements that can make or break our success. Our mindset, which refers to the beliefs, attitudes, and thoughts we hold about ourselves and the world around us, plays a pivotal role in shaping our actions, behavior, and, ultimately, our outcomes. In this subchapter, we will delve deep into the significance of mindset in personal transformation and explore how it can be harnessed to achieve remarkable results in various aspects of life.

Master Your Mindset: The Definitive Blueprint for Personal Transformation

To truly master our mindset, we must first recognize that our thoughts and beliefs hold immense power. They can either propel us forward towards our goals or hinder our progress. By adopting a growth mindset, where we see challenges as opportunities for growth and believe in our ability to learn and improve, we can unlock our true potential. This blueprint for personal transformation offers practical strategies and tools to rewire our thinking patterns and cultivate a mindset that sets us up for success in all areas of life.

Mindset Mastery for Entrepreneurs: Unlocking Your Potential to Achieve Business Success

Entrepreneurship can be a rollercoaster ride with numerous highs and lows. However, those with a resilient and entrepreneurial mindset can navigate these challenges with grace and determination. This subchapter explores successful entrepreneurs' specific mindset traits, such as embracing failure as a learning opportunity, maintaining a positive attitude in the face of adversity, and cultivating a growth-oriented mindset. By adopting these mindset principles, entrepreneurs can unlock their potential, overcome obstacles, and achieve remarkable business success.

Mindset for Financial Abundance: Cultivating a Wealth Mindset for Prosperity and Financial Freedom

Our mindset around money and abundance greatly influences our financial outcomes. Cultivating a wealth mindset involves shifting our beliefs and attitudes towards money, embracing abundance, and developing a positive relationship with wealth. This subchapter provides practical strategies for changing our money mindset, such as reframing limiting beliefs about money, practicing gratitude for our current financial situation, and adopting a long-term wealth-building mindset. By mastering our mindset for financial abundance, we can attract prosperity, achieve financial freedom, and create a life of abundance.

In conclusion, the role of mindset in personal transformation cannot be overstated. Whether it's mastering our mindset for personal growth, unlocking our potential as entrepreneurs, or cultivating a wealth mindset for financial abundance, our beliefs and attitudes shape our reality. By understanding the power of mindset and implementing practical strategies, we can unleash our inner power and achieve extraordinary results in all areas of life. So, let us embark on this transformative journey together and harness the power of mindset to create a life of purpose, fulfillment, and success.

The Science Behind Mindset and Its Impact on Success

One of the most crucial elements in the journey towards personal transformation is the power of mindset. Our mindset, beliefs, and attitudes towards ourselves and the world profoundly impact our ability to succeed in various areas of life. Whether mastering your mindset for personal growth, unlocking your potential as an entrepreneur, or cultivating a wealth mindset for financial abundance, the science behind mindset is a critical aspect to explore.

We must delve into psychology and neuroscience to truly understand the science behind mindset. These disciplines have shed light on the incredible capabilities of the human mind and how it shapes our actions, behaviors, and outcomes.

Research has shown that our mindset can determine whether we view challenges as growth opportunities or insurmountable obstacles.

One of the key concepts in understanding mindset is the idea of a fixed mindset versus a growth mindset. A fixed mindset assumes that our abilities and intelligence are fixed traits that cannot be changed. In contrast, a growth mindset believes that our abilities can be developed through dedication, effort, and learning. The impact of adopting a growth mindset is immense, as it allows individuals to embrace challenges, persist in the face of setbacks, and ultimately achieve greater levels of success.

Furthermore, neuroscience has revealed that our mindset directly impacts our brain's plasticity or ability to change and adapt. Through neuroplasticity, we can rewire our brains by challenging our existing beliefs and replacing them with more empowering ones. Individuals can create new neural pathways that support their transformation and success by intentionally cultivating a positive and growth-oriented mindset.

Mastering your mindset for personal transformation, unlocking your potential as an entrepreneur, or cultivating a wealth mindset for financial abundance requires a deep understanding of the underlying science. By harnessing the power of mindset and aligning it with specific goals, individuals can tap into their inner power and achieve remarkable results.

In this subchapter, we will explore the science behind mindset in detail, examining the psychological and neurological factors that shape our beliefs and behaviors. We will uncover strategies and techniques to cultivate a growth mindset, overcome limiting beliefs, and harness the power of neuroplasticity for personal transformation. Through real-life examples and practical exercises, readers will gain a comprehensive understanding of the science behind mindset and how to apply it to their own lives.

By mastering your mindset, you have the potential to unlock your inner power, achieve personal transformation, and create the success you desire in all areas of life.

The Difference Between a Fxed and Growth Mindset

One of the most crucial aspects of personal transformation is the difference between fixed and growth mindsets. These two mindsets shape our beliefs, attitudes, and behaviors, ultimately determining our level of success and fulfillment in life. Whether you want to master your mindset, unlock your potential as an entrepreneur, cultivate a wealth mindset, or achieve financial freedom, understanding these mindsets is paramount.

A fixed mindset is characterized by the belief that our abilities, intelligence, and talents are fixed traits that cannot be changed or developed. People with a fixed mindset tend to avoid challenges, fearing failure and the possibility of exposing their limitations. They often view effort as fruitless and believe that innate abilities determine success. Consequently, setbacks and criticism are seen as personal attacks, leading to defensiveness and a lack of resilience.

On the other hand, a growth mindset is founded on the belief that our abilities can be developed through dedication, effort, and a willingness to learn. Individuals with a growth mindset embrace challenges as opportunities for growth and see failure as a stepping stone toward success. They understand that effort is the pathway to mastery and view setbacks as valuable lessons that enable them to improve and excel.

The distinction between these mindsets has profound implications for personal transformation and success in various niches. For those seeking to master their mindset, adopting a growth mindset is essential. It empowers individuals to overcome limiting beliefs, tap into their potential, and continuously grow and evolve.

Entrepreneurs can also significantly benefit from embracing a growth mindset. Seeing challenges as opportunities makes them more resilient and adaptable to the ever-changing business landscape. A growth mindset enables them to learn from failures, pivot when necessary, and ultimately achieve long-term success.

Cultivating a growth mindset is crucial in the realm of financial abundance. By recognizing that external factors do not solely determine wealth, individuals can adopt an attitude that focuses on abundance, possibility, and continuous growth. This attitude allows them to develop the skills, knowledge, and strategies necessary to create financial freedom and prosperity.

In conclusion, understanding the difference between a fixed and growth mindset is fundamental for personal transformation in any niche. By embracing a growth mindset, individuals can unlock their potential, overcome challenges, and succeed in mastering their mindset, entrepreneurship, and cultivating financial abundance. Through the power of a growth mindset, we can unleash our inner power and truly transform our lives.

Identifying Limiting Beliefs and Negative Thought Patterns

One of the most crucial steps in our journey towards personal transformation and unlocking our inner power is identifying and addressing our limiting beliefs and negative thought patterns. These influences can hold us back from achieving our true potential and hinder our progress in various aspects of life, including personal growth, business success, and financial abundance. This subchapter will delve into recognizing and overcoming these obstacles, empowering individuals to master their mindset for personal transformation.

Limiting beliefs are deeply ingrained thoughts or ideas about ourselves, others, and the world around us. These beliefs often stem from past experiences, societal conditioning, or childhood traumas. They act as self-imposed barriers, preventing us from taking risks, pursuing our dreams, or embracing new opportunities. By identifying these limiting beliefs, we can challenge and reframe them, ultimately freeing ourselves from their restrictive grip.

Negative thought patterns, on the other hand, are recurring and pessimistic thoughts that cloud our minds and hinder our progress. These patterns can manifest as self-doubt, fear of failure, or a constant focus on potential obstacles rather than possibilities.

Recognizing these negative thought patterns can replace them with positive afirmations, constructive thinking, and empowering beliefs that propel us toward personal growth and success.

This subchapter provides individuals with practical strategies for identifying their limiting beliefs and negative thought patterns. Readers will gain valuable insights into their subconscious programming through self- reflection exercises, journaling prompts, and guided introspection. They will learn to distinguish between empowering beliefs and self-sabotaging thoughts, enabling them to make conscious choices that align with their goals and aspirations.

Moreover, this subchapter will address the specific needs of individuals in various niches, including mastering a mindset for personal transformation, mindset mastery for entrepreneurs, and cultivating a wealth mindset for financial abundance. By tailoring the content to these niches, readers will find practical applications and real-life examples that resonate with their goals and challenges.

By understanding and identifying our limiting beliefs and negative thought patterns, we can begin the transformative process of reframing our mindset and unleashing our inner power. Through this subchapter, individuals will embark on a profound journey toward personal growth, business success, and financial abundance, ultimately mastering their mindset for a life of fulfillment and achievement.

Summary

Feel free to write down any after-reading insights and thoughts

After reading this, I feel right now...

Chapter 2: Cultivating a Growth Mindset for Personal Transformation

Embracing Change and Resilience

Change is a constant in life, essential for personal growth and transformation. In our fast-paced world, adapting and embracing change is a vital skill that sets individuals apart from the rest. This subchapter will explore the significance of embracing change and developing resilience and how it can positively impact various aspects of our lives.

Mastering your mindset is crucial for individuals seeking personal transformation. It is about taking control of your thoughts and beliefs and consciously choosing to adopt a growth mindset. Embracing change is an integral part of this process. Change can be intimidating and uncomfortable, but it is through change that we can uncover our true potential. By embracing change, we open ourselves to new opportunities and possibilities for personal growth and success.

Entrepreneurs, in particular, can significantly benefit from embracing change and resilience. The business landscape constantly evolves, and entrepreneurs must adapt to stay ahead. By cultivating a mindset that sees change as an opportunity rather than a threat, entrepreneurs can navigate through challenges and setbacks with resilience. They can learn from failures, iterate their strategies, and ultimately achieve business success.

Similarly, cultivating a wealth mindset is essential for financial abundance and freedom. The ability to embrace change and adapt to new circumstances is critical in the ever-changing world of finance and investments. By developing resilience, individuals can bounce back from financial setbacks, learn from their mistakes, and make better decisions for long-term prosperity.

This subchapter will provide practical strategies and techniques for embracing change and building resilience. We will explore the power of positive thinking, visualization, and afirmations to overcome resistance to change and delve into the importance of self-care, mindfulness, and gratitude in developing resilience.

By embracing change and resilience, individuals can unlock their true potential, achieve personal transformation, and create a life of success, abundance, and fulfillment. Whether you seek personal growth, entrepreneurial success, or financial freedom, embracing change and resilience will guide you toward personal transformation. Are you ready to unleash your inner power and embrace the opportunities that change brings? Let's embark on this transformative journey together.

Developing a Positive Attitude and Optimism

In today's fast-paced and competitive world, cultivating a positive attitude and optimism is becoming increasingly essential to thrive and achieve personal transformation. A positive mindset helps us overcome challenges and setbacks and allows us to tap into our inner power and unlock our true potential. This subchapter aims to provide individuals with the tools and strategies to develop a positive attitude and cultivate optimism regardless of their chosen niche.

The first step towards developing a positive attitude is becoming aware of our thoughts and emotions. By listening to our inner dialogue, we can identify any negative or self-defeating beliefs holding us back. Once identified, we can challenge and replace these negative thoughts with positive afirmations and empowering beliefs. This process may require conscious effort and repetition but will become second nature with time.

Another critical aspect of developing a positive attitude is practicing gratitude. Gratitude allows us to shift our focus from what is lacking in our lives to what we already have. Regularly expressing gratitude for the blessings and opportunities that come our way can cultivate a sense of appreciation and contentment, which, in turn, helps us develop a more positive outlook on life.

Optimism, on the other hand, is about having a positive expectation for the future. It is the belief that things will work out for the best, even in adversity. Cultivating optimism involves reframing challenges as opportunities for growth and learning. By adopting a solution-oriented mindset and seeking out the lessons in every situation, we can maintain a positive outlook and remain resilient in the face of obstacles.

It is also crucial to surround ourselves with positive influences to develop a positive attitude and optimism. This may involve seeking out mentors, joining supportive communities, or engaging in activities that uplift and inspire us. By positively surrounding ourselves, we can create an environment that nourishes and reinforces our growth mindset.

In conclusion, developing a positive attitude and optimism is essential for personal transformation in any niche. Individuals can unleash their inner power and succeed in all areas of their lives by cultivating a positive mindset, practicing gratitude, and adopting an optimistic outlook. Remember, our mindset is the key to unlocking our true potential, and by mastering it, we can create a life of abundance, prosperity, and fulfillment.

Setting and Achieving Goals with a Growth Mindset

Setting goals is not enough in today's fast-paced and competitive world; we must also cultivate a growth mindset to achieve them. The power of our mindset cannot be underestimated when it comes to personal transformation. This subchapter will explore how to unleash our inner power by mastering our mindset, explicitly focusing on setting and achieving goals with a growth mindset.

A growth mindset is the belief that our abilities and intelligence can be developed through dedication, hard work, and a willingness to learn from failure. It thrives on challenges, embraces setbacks as opportunities for growth, and seeks new ways to improve. By adopting a growth mindset, we can overcome obstacles, push our limits, and achieve levels of success we never thought possible.

When setting goals with a growth mindset, it is essential to be specific and realistic. Setting vague or unrealistic goals can lead to frustration and a lack of motivation. Instead, we should define our goals in clear and measurable terms, ensuring they are attainable within a reasonable timeframe. We can maintain momentum and build confidence by breaking down larger goals into smaller, manageable steps.

Another crucial aspect of setting and achieving goals with a growth mindset is to embrace failure as a stepping stone to success. Failure is not a reflection of our abilities but rather an opportunity for growth and learning. Reframing failure as feedback allows us to adjust our strategies, learn from our mistakes, and continue moving forward. A growth mindset understands that setbacks are temporary and that success is achieved through perseverance and resilience.

To cultivate a growth mindset, it is essential to surround ourselves with a supportive network. Seek mentors, coaches, or like-minded individuals who can provide guidance, encouragement, and accountability. By surrounding ourselves with people with a growth mindset, we can tap into their knowledge, experience, and positive energy, pushing us to reach new heights.

In conclusion, setting and achieving goals with a growth mindset is a powerful tool for personal transformation. By embracing challenges, setting realistic goals, learning from failure, and surrounding ourselves with a supportive network, we can unleash our inner power and achieve remarkable success. Whether it is mastering our mindset for personal transformation, unlocking our potential for business success, or cultivating a wealth mindset for financial abundance, adopting a growth mindset is the key to unlocking our true potential. Start today, set your goals, and let your growth mindset propel you to incredible achievements.

Overcoming Fear and Embracing Failure as a Learning Opportunity

Fear and failure are two of the most common obstacles individuals encounter on their journey to personal transformation. In mastering your mindset and unlocking your potential, it is crucial to understand that fear and failure are not enemies to be avoided but opportunities for growth and learning.

Fear is a natural human emotion that often arises when we step outside our comfort zones. It can be paralyzing, causing us to hesitate and doubt ourselves. However, by embracing and acknowledging fear as a sign of growth, we can overcome its grip and move forward confidently.

One key to overcoming fear is to reframe it as excitement. Instead of allowing fear to hold us back, we can view it as a signal that we are on the right path toward personal transformation. By shifting our mindset and embracing fear as a positive force, we can harness its energy to propel us forward rather than allowing it to hinder our progress.

Similarly, failure is often seen as a negative outcome, something to be avoided at all costs. However, failure is an essential part of the learning process. It provides valuable feedback and teaches us what does not work, allowing us to refine our approach and ultimately achieve success.

Adopting a growth mindset is vital to embracing failure as a learning opportunity. Instead of viewing failure as a reflection of our worth or abilities, we can see it as a stepping stone toward personal growth and improvement. By reframing failure as a necessary part of the journey, we can let go of the fear of failure and instead focus on the valuable lessons it offers.

In the niches of mastering a mindset for personal transformation, mindset mastery for entrepreneurs, and a mindset for financial abundance, the ability to overcome fear and embrace failure is essential.

Entrepreneurs face numerous challenges and setbacks on their path to success, and a resilient mindset is crucial to navigate these obstacles. Similarly, cultivating a wealth mindset requires taking risks, overcoming fear, and learning from failure.

In conclusion, fear and failure are not enemies to be avoided but opportunities for growth and learning. By embracing fear as a sign of growth and reframing failure as a learning opportunity, individuals can unleash their inner power and master their mindset for personal transformation, entrepreneurial success, and financial abundance.

Summary

Feel free to write down any after-reading insights and thoughts

After reading this, I feel right now...

Chapter 3: Mastering Your Mindset for Entrepreneurial Success

The Entrepreneurial Mindset: Traits and Characteristics

In today's rapidly changing world, cultivating an entrepreneurial mindset has become imperative for individuals seeking personal transformation and success in various niches, such as mastering mindset, entrepreneurship, and financial abundance. In this subchapter, "Unleashing Your Inner Power: Mastering Your Mindset for Personal Transformation," we delve into the traits and characteristics defining an entrepreneurial mindset.

First and foremost, an entrepreneurial mindset is characterized by a strong sense of self-belief and confidence. Entrepreneurs understand that they have the power to shape their destinies and are not afraid to take risks or step outside their comfort zones. They possess a burning desire to achieve their goals and are willing to put in the necessary effort and persistence to make them a reality.

Another key trait of the entrepreneurial mindset is a relentless drive for innovation. Entrepreneurs constantly seek new opportunities, challenge the status quo, and solve problems creatively. They embrace change and view it as an opportunity for growth and improvement. This mindset allows them to stay ahead of the curve, adapt to new technologies and trends, and seize untapped markets.

Entrepreneurs also have a proactive and action-oriented mindset. They do not wait for opportunities to come to them; instead, they actively seek them out and take decisive action. They are not discouraged by failure but rather see it as a learning experience and an opportunity for growth. This resilience and ability to bounce back from setbacks is a crucial characteristic of the entrepreneurial mindset.

Furthermore, entrepreneurs possess excellent problem-solving skills and a strong sense of resourcefulness. They are adept at identifying challenges and finding creative solutions to overcome them. They are not afraid to ask for help or guidance from mentors and experts in their fields. This willingness to learn and constantly improve sets successful entrepreneurs apart.

In conclusion, cultivating an entrepreneurial mindset is essential for personal transformation and success in various niches, such as mastering mindset, entrepreneurship, and financial abundance. Traits such as self- belief, innovation, proactivity, resilience, and problem-solving skills define this mindset. By embracing these characteristics and adopting an entrepreneurial mindset, individuals can unlock their full potential and achieve their goals, whether it be personal, professional, or financial.

Developing a Wnning Mindset for Business Growth

A winning mindset is crucial for achieving growth and success in the fast-paced and competitive business world. This subchapter will explore the fundamental principles and strategies for cultivating a winning attitude and unlocking your potential for business growth.

Embrace a Growth Mindset: Adopting a growth mindset is the first step towards developing a winning attitude. Understand that your abilities and intelligence can be developed through dedication, hard work, and continuous learning. Embrace challenges as opportunities to learn and grow, and view failures as valuable lessons that can propel you toward success.

Set Clear Goals: Clearly define your business goals and create a roadmap. Break down your goals into actionable steps and set realistic deadlines. A clear vision and direction lets you stay focused and motivated, even in the face of obstacles

Cultivate a Positive Attitude: A positive attitude is essential for resilience and overcoming challenges. Surround yourself with positive influences, practice gratitude, and replace negative thoughts with positive afirmations. Remember, your mindset determines your reality, so choose to see the opportunities and possibilities in every situation.

Develop Emotional Intelligence: Emotional intelligence is the ability to understand and manage your emotions and those of others. You can effectively communicate, build strong relationships, and make sound decisions by cultivating emotional intelligence. This skill set is invaluable in business, where collaboration and effective leadership are essential for growth.

Take Calculated Risks: To achieve business growth, you must be willing to step out of your comfort zone and take calculated risks. Understand that failure is a part of the journey, and use it as an opportunity to learn and improve. Trust your instincts, gather relevant information, and make informed decisions that align with your goals and values.

Practice Persistence and Resilience: Business growth is not linear, and setbacks are inevitable. Develop a mindset of persistence and resilience, and view challenges as temporary roadblocks rather than permanent obstacles. Learn from your mistakes, adapt to changing circumstances, and keep moving forward with determination and perseverance.

By adopting these principles and strategies, you can cultivate a winning mindset to drive your personal and professional growth. Remember, success in business starts from within, and with the right mindset, you can unleash your full potential and achieve extraordinary results.

Building Confidence and Overcoming Imposter Syndrome

Confidence is the key to unlocking your inner power and achieving personal transformation. It is the fuel that propels you forward, allowing you to conquer your fears and overcome any challenges that come your way.

However, many individuals struggle with a familiar obstacle known as imposter syndrome. This subchapter will delve deep into the intricacies of building confidence and provide practical strategies to overcome imposter syndrome.

Imposter syndrome is a psychological pattern in which individuals doubt their accomplishments and persistently fear being exposed as frauds. It affects people from all walks of life, including entrepreneurs, professionals seeking personal transformation, and those striving for financial abundance. The good news is that imposter syndrome can be conquered, and confidence can be built.

To begin your journey towards building confidence, it is essential to recognize and challenge your self-doubt. Understand that everyone experiences self-doubt, but it does not define your worth or abilities. Embrace your unique qualities and past accomplishments as they prove your capabilities.

Next, it is crucial to adopt a growth mindset. Embrace challenges as opportunities for growth and view failures as stepping stones towards success. By reframing your perspective, you can transform setbacks into valuable learning experiences.

Another powerful strategy to overcome imposter syndrome is to surround yourself with a supportive network. Seek out mentors, coaches, or like-minded individuals who can provide guidance and encouragement. Remember, you are not alone in your journey; having a solid support system can make all the difference.

Self-care and self-compassion are essential in building confidence and overcoming imposter syndrome. Take time for self-reflection, engage in activities that bring you joy, and celebrate small victories. Treat yourself with kindness and understanding, just like a close friend.

Lastly, embrace the power of afirmations and visualization. Create positive afirmations that reflect your strengths and goals and repeat them daily. Visualize confidently, achieving your desired outcomes and letting these visualizations manifest into reality.

In conclusion, building confidence and overcoming imposter syndrome is a crucial step towards personal transformation. By challenging your self-doubt, adopting a growth mindset, surrounding yourself with support, practicing self-care, and harnessing the power of afirmations and visualization, you can unleash your inner power and achieve success in any niche of life, be it mastering your mindset, achieving business success, or cultivating wealth and financial freedom. Remember, you are capable, deserving, and more than enough. Embrace your true potential and let your confidence soar.

Effective Communication and Influencing Others with Your Mindset

Effective communication is a powerful tool that can positively influence others and transform your personal and professional life. This subchapter will explore the connection between your mindset and your ability to communicate and influence others effectively.

Your mindset is the foundation of your thoughts, beliefs, and attitudes. It shapes your world perception and determines how you interact with others. Regarding communication, your mindset plays a crucial role in your ability to connect with others and influence them positively.

To become an effective communicator, you must first cultivate a growth mindset. This mindset is characterized by believing in your ability to learn and grow.

It allows you to embrace challenges, persist in the face of setbacks, and see failure as an opportunity for growth. When you approach communication with a growth mindset, you are more open to feedback, willing to listen to others, and eager to learn from their perspectives.

Another critical aspect of effective communication is self-awareness. Understanding your thoughts, emotions, and biases enables you to communicate authentically and empathetically. By being aware of your mindset, you can recognize when it may limit your ability to connect with others. This self-awareness allows you to make conscious choices about communicating and positively influencing those around you.

Influencing others with your mindset also requires the development of strong interpersonal skills. These skills include active listening, empathy, and adapting your communication style to different individuals and situations. By actively listening to others and genuinely understanding their needs and desires, you can tailor your message to resonate with them on a deeper level.

Furthermore, cultivating a mindset of abundance and positivity can significantly enhance your ability to influence others. By adopting an attitude of abundance, you see opportunities instead of obstacles and believe there is enough success and prosperity for everyone. This mindset allows you to inspire and motivate others, creating a ripple effect of positive change.

In conclusion, effective communication and influencing others with your mindset are essential skills for personal transformation and success in various niches. By cultivating a growth mindset, practicing self- awareness, and developing strong interpersonal skills, you can positively harness the power of communication to impact your personal and professional life. Remember, your mindset is the key to unlocking your inner power and transforming your life.

Summary

Feel free to write down any after-reading insights and thoughts

After reading this, I feel right now...

Chapter 4: Unleashing Your Wealth Mindset for Fnancial Abundance

Understanding the Connection Between Mindset and Wealth

In today's fast-paced and ever-changing world, it is becoming increasingly clear that success and wealth go hand in hand with one's mindset. How we think and perceive the world around us profoundly impacts our ability to achieve financial abundance and prosperity. This subchapter will explore the fundamental connection between mindset and wealth and how mastering your mindset can unlock your inner power for personal transformation.

Master Your Mindset: The Definitive Blueprint for Personal Transformation

To truly master your mindset and unleash your inner power, it is crucial to understand its role in achieving personal transformation. Your mindset determines how you view the world and shapes your beliefs, attitudes, and actions. By cultivating a growth mindset, where you believe in your ability to learn and grow, you open yourself up to endless possibilities for success and wealth.

Mindset Mastery for Entrepreneurs: Unlocking Your Potential to Achieve Business Success

Mindset mastery is the key to achieving business success for entrepreneurs. Entrepreneurs face numerous challenges and obstacles along their journey, and their mindset determines how they navigate these hurdles. By adopting an entrepreneurial mindset, which includes resilience, adaptability, and a willingness to take calculated risks, entrepreneurs can overcome setbacks and propel their businesses to new heights of success.

Mindset for Financial Abundance: Cultivating a Wealth Mindset for Prosperity and Financial Freedom

Cultivating a wealth mindset is essential for achieving financial abundance and freedom. A wealth mindset involves shifting your focus from scarcity and limitations to abundance and possibilities. It is about adopting a positive and proactive attitude towards money and developing healthy money habits. By believing in your ability to attract and create wealth, you open yourself to a world of opportunities and prosperity.

Understanding the connection between mindset and wealth is the first step towards unlocking your inner power and transforming your life. By mastering your mindset, you can overcome self-limiting beliefs, develop resilience in the face of challenges, and create a positive and abundant mindset that attracts wealth and success. Whether you seek personal transformation, business success, or financial abundance, harnessing the power of your mindset is the key to unlocking your true potential.

In the following chapters, we will delve deeper into specific strategies and techniques for mastering your mindset in each of these niches. By combining the power of mindset with practical tools and insights, you will be well on your way to unleashing your inner power and achieving the personal transformation, business success, and financial abundance you desire. Get ready to embark on a transformative journey that will revolutionize your life and propel you toward the life of your dreams.

Overcoming Scarcity Thinking and Embracing Abundance

One of the key obstacles we often encounter in our journey toward personal transformation is scarcity thinking. Scarcity thinking is a mindset that revolves around lack, limitations, and the fear of not having enough. It keeps us trapped in a cycle of negativity, preventing us from achieving our true potential and experiencing abundance in all aspects of life.

This subchapter aims to help individuals across various niches, including Master Your Mindset, Mindset Mastery for Entrepreneurs, and Mindset for Financial Abundance, to break free from scarcity thinking and embrace the abundance that awaits them.

The first step in overcoming scarcity thinking is to recognize its presence in our lives. We must acknowledge the negative thought patterns that arise when we focus on what we lack rather than what we have. By becoming aware of these thoughts, we can challenge and reframe them.

Next, we need to shift our mindset from scarcity to abundance. This involves adopting an attitude of gratitude and appreciation for the blessings we already have. By focusing on the positive aspects of our lives, we open ourselves up to attract more abundance and opportunities.

To truly embrace abundance, we must also release any limiting beliefs that hold us back. These beliefs often stem from past experiences or societal conditioning, creating a self-imposed barrier to success. By identifying and challenging these beliefs, we can replace them with empowering thoughts that support our journey toward abundance.

Furthermore, it is essential to surround ourselves with like-minded individuals who also strive for abundance. By building a supportive network, we can exchange ideas, learn from one another, and hold each other accountable for maintaining a positive mindset.

Lastly, embracing abundance requires taking inspired action. We must proactively seek opportunities, take calculated risks, and step out of our comfort zones. By doing so, we align ourselves with the flow of abundance and open doors that were previously closed.

In conclusion, overcoming scarcity and embracing abundance is a transformative process that can lead to personal and financial growth. By shifting our mindset, releasing limiting beliefs, and taking inspired action, we can unleash our inner power and attract abundance in all areas of our lives. So, let us let go of scarcity and embrace the limitless possibilities that await us.

Developing a Money Mindset for Fnancial Success

Financial success has become a key measure of personal achievement in today's fast-paced world. However, many individuals struggle to attain and maintain the desired prosperity. The truth is that achieving financial success goes beyond just having a good job or making intelligent investments. It requires a specific mindset that enables individuals to develop a healthy relationship with money and cultivate a wealth mindset.

This subchapter will explore the essential steps to developing a money mindset for financial success. Whether you are an entrepreneur aiming to achieve business success, an individual seeking personal transformation, or someone striving for financial abundance and freedom, mastering your mindset is the key to prosperity.

Firstly, we will explore the importance of understanding your relationship with money. Your mindset towards money is deeply rooted in your upbringing, beliefs, and experiences. By examining these factors, you can identify any limiting beliefs or negative associations holding you back from financial success. You can reframe these beliefs and develop a positive money mindset through introspection and self-awareness.

Next, we will discuss the power of goal setting and visualization in creating financial abundance. By setting clear financial goals and visualizing yourself already achieving them, you align your subconscious mind with your desired outcomes. This process allows you to attract opportunities, make better financial decisions, and take inspired action toward your goals.

Furthermore, we will explore the importance of financial education and continuous learning. Developing a money mindset involves understanding the principles of wealth creation, investing, and financial management. By seeking knowledge and staying informed about financial matters, you can make informed decisions that lead to long-term economic success.

Lastly, we will emphasize the significance of gratitude and abundance mentality. Gratitude opens the doors to abundance by shifting your focus from scarcity to abundance. By appreciating the resources you already have and expressing gratitude for the money you receive, you invite more wealth into your life.

In conclusion, developing a money mindset for financial success is crucial in achieving prosperity and economic freedom. Understanding your relationship with money, setting clear goals, continuously learning, and cultivating gratitude can transform your mindset and unlock your inner power for financial abundance. Whether you are an entrepreneur, an individual seeking personal transformation, or someone striving for economic freedom, this subchapter will provide the tools and guidance necessary to develop a money mindset leading to lasting financial success.

Practicing Wealth Consciousness and Attracting Prosperity

One key aspect often overlooked in the journey of personal transformation is the power of wealth consciousness. Many believe that financial abundance solely depends on external factors such as luck or hard work. However, true prosperity begins from within by cultivating a wealth mindset.

Mastering Your Mindset for Personal Transformation, as the title of this book suggests, is a comprehensive guide that empowers individuals to unlock their inner power. This subchapter, "Practicing Wealth Consciousness and Attracting Prosperity," delves into the techniques and strategies required to cultivate a wealth mindset and attract financial abundance.

Mindset mastery cannot be emphasized enough for entrepreneurs seeking business success. Developing a wealth consciousness allows entrepreneurs to align their thoughts, beliefs, and actions with their financial goals. By shifting their mindset from scarcity to abundance, they can attract opportunities, make sound decisions, and easily overcome obstacles.

Similarly, individuals interested in cultivating a wealth mindset for prosperity and financial freedom will find valuable insights in this subchapter. It explores the power of positive afirmations, visualization, and gratitude as tools for reprogramming the subconscious mind to attract wealth and abundance. Additionally, it provides practical exercises and techniques to overcome limiting beliefs, develop a money mindset, and create a financial plan for long-term prosperity.

Furthermore, the subchapter delves into wealth consciousness and its connection to the law of attraction. By understanding the principles of this universal law, individuals can harness their thoughts and emotions to manifest their desired financial outcomes. It highlights the importance of maintaining a positive mindset, practicing daily afirmations, and taking inspired action to attract prosperity.

In conclusion, "Practicing Wealth Consciousness and Attracting Prosperity" is a vital subchapter within the book "Unleashing Your Inner Power: Mastering Your Mindset for Personal Transformation." It empowers individuals in various niches, including entrepreneurs and those seeking financial abundance. By implementing the techniques and strategies outlined in this subchapter, readers can cultivate a wealth mindset, unlock their inner power, and attract prosperity into their lives.

Summary

Feel free to write down any after-reading insights and thoughts

After reading this, I feel right now...

Chapter 5: Harnessing the Power of Visualization and Affirmations

The Science Behind Vsualization and Its Impact on Mindset

Mastering your mindset is crucial in the journey towards personal transformation. It is the foundation upon which all other aspects of personal growth are built. One powerful tool that can significantly impact your mindset is visualization. This subchapter explores the science behind visualization and its profound effects on shaping a positive and success-oriented mindset.

Visualization, or mental imagery, creates vivid pictures or scenes in your mind. It involves using your imagination to visualize specific goals, dreams, or desired outcomes. While visualization may seem simple, scientific research backs its impact on the mind.

When we visualize, our brain activates the same neural pathways as when we experience the imagined scenario. Numerous studies have observed this phenomenon, including those using brain imaging technology. The brain cannot differentiate between an authentic experience and a vividly imagined one. This means that by consistently visualizing positive outcomes, we can rewire our brains to believe in our ability to achieve them.

Visualization also influences our emotions and beliefs. When we vividly imagine achieving our goals, our brain releases neurotransmitters associated with pleasure and reward. This leads to increased motivation, focus, and confidence. As we repeatedly visualize success, our belief in our capabilities strengthens, fostering a positive mindset essential for personal transformation.

Furthermore, visualization enhances our ability to problem-solve and overcome obstacles. We mentally rehearse challenging situations and activate the brain's creative problem-solving centers. This helps us develop strategies and solutions to navigate real-life barriers more effectively.

Visualization is invaluable for individuals seeking personal transformation in various niches, such as mindset mastery, entrepreneurial success, or financial abundance. By consistently visualizing the desired outcomes in these areas, individuals can align their subconscious minds with their conscious goals.

In "Unleashing Your Inner Power: Mastering Your Mindset for Personal Transformation," we delve deeper into the science behind visualization and its practical applications. We explore various techniques and exercises that can help individuals harness the power of visualization to unlock their true potential.

Whether you aspire to master your mindset, achieve entrepreneurial success, or cultivate a wealth mindset, visualization can be a game-changer. By understanding the science behind visualization and incorporating it into your daily practice, you can reprogram your mind for success and create your desired life.

Creating Powerful Affirmations for Personal Transformation

In the journey of personal transformation, one powerful tool that can help individuals unlock their inner power and master their mindset is afirmations. Afirmations are positive statements that, when repeated consistently, can reprogram the subconscious mind and align it with our desires and goals. By harnessing the power of afirmations, individuals can cultivate a mindset that propels them towards success, whether in personal growth, entrepreneurship, or financial abundance.

To create powerful afirmations, following a few fundamental principles is essential. First, afirmations should always be stated in the present tense. Doing so sends a clear message to our subconscious mind that our desired reality is already happening.

For example, instead of saying, "I will become successful," a powerful afirmation would be, "I am successful in all areas of my life."

Secondly, afirmations should be positive and uplifting. They should focus on what we want rather than what we want to avoid. By positively framing our afirmations, we attract positive energy and opportunities. For instance, instead of saying, "I am not afraid of failure," a powerful afirmation would be, "I embrace challenges and learn from every experience."

Another critical aspect of creating powerful afirmations is making them specific and detailed. When we are clear about our desires, our subconscious mind can work towards manifesting them more effectively. For example, instead of saying, "I am financially abundant," a powerful afirmation would be, "I am attracting multiple streams of income effortlessly and enjoying financial abundance."

Consistency is also crucial when it comes to afirmations. To harness their power, individuals must repeat their afirmations daily, ideally multiple times. By doing so, the afirmations become ingrained in our subconscious mind, transforming our thoughts, beliefs, and actions.

In the book "Unleashing Your Inner Power: Mastering Your Mindset for Personal Transformation," individuals in the niches of mastering mindset, mindset mastery for entrepreneurs, and mindset for financial abundance will find a comprehensive guide on creating powerful afirmations. They will learn how to craft afirmations that resonate with their specific goals and desires and how to integrate them into their daily routine for maximum impact. With these tools, readers can unlock their inner power and transform their lives unimaginably.

Utilizing Vsualization and Affirmations for Goal Achievement

Mastering our mindset is crucial in the journey towards personal transformation and achieving our goals. Our thoughts and beliefs shape our reality, and by harnessing the power of visualization and afirmations, we can unlock our inner power and manifest our desires.

Visualization is a powerful tool that allows us to create a mental image of our desired outcome. By vividly imagining ourselves already achieving our goals, we activate our subconscious mind and align it with our conscious intentions. This process helps us tap into our creative potential and boosts our motivation and confidence.

Engaging all our senses is essential for effective visualization. Close your eyes and imagine yourself in the specific situation you desire. What do you see, hear, smell, taste, and feel? Visualize the details, emotions, and positive outcomes. Immerse yourself in this mental image and hold onto it, believing it is already confirmed.

Afirmations complement visualization by reinforcing positive beliefs and programming our subconscious mind for success. Afirmations are positive statements that reflect our goals and aspirations. By repeating these afirmations regularly, we replace limiting beliefs with empowering ones, shaping our mindset for achievement.

When creating afirmations, ensure they are in the present tense, use positive language, and are aligned with your values and goals. For example, instead of saying, "I will be financially abundant," say, "I am financially abundant, and money flows to me effortlessly." Repeat these afirmations daily, ideally in front of a mirror, so you can connect with your reflection and internalize the words.

Combine visualization and afirmations with gratitude to enhance their impact. Expressing gratitude for what you already have and your progress towards your goals amplifies the positive energy and attracts more abundance into your life. Incorporate gratitude into your visualization and afirmations, appreciating the journey and the support you receive.

Remember that visualization and afirmations are not a substitute for action. They serve as a catalyst for transformation and provide the mental clarity and focus needed to take inspired action toward your goals. Use them daily to align your thoughts, beliefs, and actions, and watch as your mindset shifts, obstacles dissolve, and your goals become reality.

Whether you are seeking personal transformation, business success, or financial abundance, the power of visualization and afirmations is available to you. You can unlock your true potential and create your desired life by harnessing your inner power and mastering your mindset. Start utilizing visualization and afirmations today, and watch your dreams unfold before your eyes.

Incorporating Vsualization and Affirmations into Daily Practice

Visualization and afirmations are powerful tools that help individuals unlock their inner power and transform their lives. Whether you seek personal growth, business success, or financial abundance, mastering your mindset through visualization and afirmations is essential.

In the book Unleashing Your Inner Power: Mastering Your Mindset for Personal Transformation, we delve into the profound impact that visualization and afirmations can have on one's life. Incorporating these practices into one's daily routine can create a blueprint for personal transformation and unlock one's true potential.

Visualization is the process of creating vivid mental images of your desired outcomes. By visualizing your goals, dreams, and aspirations, you effectively program your subconscious mind to manifest them into reality. This practice helps to align your thoughts, beliefs, and actions with your desired outcomes, making them more attainable.

Incorporating visualization into your daily practice can be as simple as setting aside a few minutes daily to visualize your goals. Find a quiet space, close your eyes, and imagine yourself already achieving what you desire. Engage all your senses and feel the emotions associated with your success. The more detailed and vivid your visualization, the more its impact will be more powerful.

Afirmations, on the other hand, are positive statements that reinforce your beliefs and aspirations. Repeating afirmations regularly can reprogram your subconscious mind and replace negative thoughts and limiting beliefs with empowering ones. Afirmations help to cultivate a positive mindset, enhance self-confidence, and attract abundance into your life.

To incorporate afirmations into your daily practice, create a list of positive statements that resonate with your goals and desires. Repeat these afirmations aloud or in your mind, preferably in front of a mirror, to reinforce their impact. Make it a habit to practice afirmations daily, ideally in the morning or before bed, to set the tone for a positive and successful day.

Whether you seek personal growth, an entrepreneur aiming for business success, or someone striving for financial abundance, incorporating visualization and afirmations into your daily practice is crucial. Mastering your mindset through these powerful tools can overcome limiting beliefs, reprogram your subconscious mind, and unleash your inner power.

"Unleashing Your Inner Power: Mastering Your Mindset for Personal Transformation" provides a definitive blueprint for incorporating visualization and afirmations into your daily routine. The book offers practical exercises, tips, and guidance to help you harness the full potential of visualization and afirmations.

Through consistent practice, you can master your mindset and transform every aspect of your life. Get ready to unleash your inner power and create your desired life.

Summary

Feel free to write down any after-reading insights and thoughts

After reading this, I feel right now...

____

____

____

____

____

____

____

Chapter 6: Nurturing a Positive Mindset for Emotional Well-Being

The Connection Between Mindset and Emotional Resilience

In today's fast-paced and ever-changing world, emotional resilience has become crucial for individuals seeking personal transformation, entrepreneurial success, and financial abundance. Your mindset, or how you perceive and interpret the world around you, determines your emotional resilience.

Emotional resilience refers to your ability to adapt and bounce back from dificult situations, setbacks, and challenges. The mental and emotional strength allows you to remain calm, focused, and confident when facing adversity. Emotional resilience is essential for personal growth, business success, and financial freedom.

Your mindset serves as the foundation for emotional resilience. It encompasses your beliefs, attitudes, and thoughts, which shape how you perceive and respond to various situations. A growth mindset, characterized by a belief in one's ability to learn and grow, is essential for building emotional resilience. It enables you to embrace challenges, learn from failures, and maintain a positive outlook despite adversity.

Mastering your mindset for personal transformation requires cultivating self-awareness and practicing mindfulness. You can identify negative or limiting beliefs that may hinder your emotional resilience by understanding your thoughts and emotions. Through mindfulness, you can observe your thoughts without judgment, allowing you to reframe negative thinking patterns and adopt a more positive and empowering mindset.

Mindset mastery is equally vital for entrepreneurs seeking business success. The entrepreneurial journey is filled with uncertainties, risks, and obstacles. Entrepreneurs may quickly become overwhelmed, discouraged, or give up without a resilient mindset.

By developing emotional resilience through a growth mindset, entrepreneurs can confidently navigate challenges, adapt to changes, and persist in pursuing their goals and visions.

Similarly, cultivating a wealth mindset is crucial for individuals seeking financial abundance and freedom. A scarcity mindset, characterized by a fear of scarcity and a belief in limited resources, can hinder one's ability to attract and create wealth. By adopting an abundance mindset and cultivating positive beliefs about money and abundance, individuals can overcome financial challenges, attract opportunities, and develop a life of prosperity and economic freedom.

In conclusion, the connection between mindset and emotional resilience is undeniable. Your mindset influences how you perceive and respond to challenges and setbacks, ultimately determining your level of emotional resilience. Developing a growth mindset, practicing mindfulness, and cultivating positive beliefs can enhance your emotional resilience and unlock your inner power for personal transformation, entrepreneurial success, and financial abundance. Mastering your mindset is the blueprint for achieving these goals and creating a fulfilling and prosperous life.

Strategies for Cultivating Positivity and Gratitude

Introduction:

Cultivating positivity and gratitude is a powerful tool in the journey towards personal transformation. It can unlock your inner power and help you master your mindset. By adopting these strategies, you can create a mindset conducive to success in your personal life, business endeavors, or financial goals.

This subchapter will explore practical strategies for cultivating positivity and gratitude and how they can benefit individuals in various niches, including Master Your Mindset, Mindset Mastery for Entrepreneurs, and Mindset for Financial Abundance.

The Power of Positive Thinking:

Positive thinking is crucial to cultivating positivity and gratitude. It involves consciously shifting your focus toward positive thoughts, emotions, and experiences. By practicing positive afirmations, visualizations, and gratitude exercises, you can naturally rewire your brain to gravitate toward positivity.

Gratitude Practice:

Gratitude is a transformative practice that involves acknowledging and appreciating the blessings in your life. By regularly expressing gratitude for the things you have, the people around you, and even the challenges you've faced, you can cultivate a mindset of abundance and attract more positivity into your life.

Surround Yourself with Positive Influences:

To cultivate positivity and gratitude, it is crucial to surround yourself with like-minded individuals who radiate positivity. Seek mentors, coaches, or communities that support your personal growth journey and provide a positive environment for you to thrive.

Mindfulness and Self-awareness:

Mindfulness and self-awareness can help you identify negative thought patterns and replace them with positive ones. You can consciously choose positive perspectives and responses by being present in the moment and observing your thoughts without judgment.

Celebrate Small Wins:

Recognize and celebrate your achievements, no matter how small they may seem. By acknowledging your progress and giving yourself credit for your accomplishments, you reinforce positive beliefs about your abilities and build a resilient mindset.

Practice Self-care:

Self-care is an essential component of cultivating positivity and gratitude. Prioritize activities that nourish your mind, body, and soul, such as exercise, meditation, spending time in nature, or engaging in hobbies that bring you joy. Taking care of yourself allows you to maintain a positive mindset and handle challenges gracefully.

Conclusion:

By implementing these strategies for cultivating positivity and gratitude, individuals in various niches can unlock their inner power, master their mindset, achieve business success, and develop financial abundance. Remember, positivity and gratitude are attitudes and powerful tools that can shape your reality and transform your life. Embrace these practices, and unleash your inner power to create your desired life.

Managing Stress and Overcoming Negative Emotions

In today's fast-paced and demanding world, stress and negative emotions can easily overwhelm us, hindering our personal growth and success. However, by managing stress and overcoming negative emotions, we can unleash our inner power and master our mindset for personal transformation. This subchapter explores effective strategies and techniques to help individuals in various niches, including mastering mindset, mindset mastery for entrepreneurs, and mindset for financial abundance.

Understanding Stress and Negative Emotions

Stress and negative emotions are natural responses to our challenges and pressures. By understanding their impact on our mental, emotional, and physical well-being, we can gain insight into managing them effectively.

Developing Resilience

Resilience is the ability to bounce back from adversity, and it plays a crucial role in managing stress and overcoming negative emotions. This subchapter provides practical tips and exercises to cultivate resilience, empowering individuals to navigate challenges with greater ease and grace.

Mindfulness and Meditation

Mindfulness and meditation are powerful tools for managing stress and negative emotions. By practicing mindfulness, individuals can develop an awareness of their thoughts and emotions, allowing them to respond rather than react. This subchapter explores various mindfulness and meditation techniques tailored to the specific needs of individuals in different niches.

Emotional Intelligence

Emotional intelligence is the ability to recognize and manage one's own emotions and the emotions of others. By enhancing emotional intelligence, individuals can effectively manage stress and negative emotions, leading to healthier relationships and improved decision-making.

Cognitive Restructuring

Cognitive restructuring involves identifying and challenging negative thought patterns and replacing them with more positive and empowering beliefs. This subchapter provides step-by-step guidance on how individuals can reframe their thoughts and overcome self-limiting beliefs.

Self-Care and Wellness

Self-care and wellness are essential for managing stress and negative emotions. This subchapter explores various self-care practices, such as exercise, nutrition, sleep, and relaxation techniques, that individuals can incorporate into their daily routines to enhance their well-being.

Seeking Support

Sometimes, managing stress and overcoming negative emotions can be challenging on our own. This subchapter emphasizes the importance of seeking support from trusted friends, family members, or even professional therapists to help individuals navigate and overcome their emotional challenges effectively.

By implementing the strategies and techniques outlined in this subchapter, individuals can effectively manage stress, overcome negative emotions, and unleash their inner power to achieve personal transformation. Whether individuals seek to master their mindset, achieve business success as entrepreneurs, or cultivate a wealth mindset for financial abundance, these tools will empower them to navigate life's challenges with resilience, positivity, and success.

Practicing Self-Compassion and Mindfulness for Emotional Well-Being

In today's fast-paced world, it's easy to get caught up in the hustle and bustle of everyday life. As individuals striving for personal transformation, business success, and financial abundance, it's crucial to prioritize our emotional well-being. This subchapter will delve into the powerful practices of self-compassion and mindfulness, which can significantly enhance our mindset and propel us towards our goals.

Self-compassion extends kindness and understanding towards ourselves during struggle, failure, or pain. It involves treating ourselves with the same care and compassion we would offer a loved one. By embracing self-compassion, we can cultivate a positive and nurturing relationship with ourselves, which is essential for personal growth.

In the context of mastering our mindset, self-compassion is a powerful tool for overcoming self-doubt and limiting beliefs. When we encounter challenges or setbacks, instead of beating ourselves up or engaging in negative self-talk, we can choose to be kind and gentle. By acknowledging our humanity and accepting our imperfections, we can foster a mindset that is resilient and open to growth.

On the other hand, mindfulness is the practice of being fully present and aware of the present moment without judgment. It involves paying attention to our thoughts, emotions, and physical sensations without getting caught up in them. By cultivating mindfulness, we can develop greater self-awareness and become more attuned to our inner workings.

For entrepreneurs, mindfulness is a game-changer. It lets us focus on the task, make clear decisions, and effectively manage stress. By training our minds to be present, we can avoid getting overwhelmed by the numerous demands of running a business and instead approach challenges with clarity and calmness.

Furthermore, developing a mindfulness practice can significantly contribute to our financial abundance. By being fully present in our economic decisions, we can make more informed choices and avoid impulsive or emotionally driven actions.

Mindfulness can also help us identify and challenge scarcity or limiting beliefs around money, paving the way for a wealth mindset and financial freedom.

In conclusion, incorporating self-compassion and mindfulness into our lives is crucial for our emotional well- being and personal transformation. By practicing self-compassion, we can foster a mindset that is supportive and growth-oriented, while mindfulness allows us to stay present and make conscious choices. Whether striving for personal transformation, entrepreneurial success, or financial abundance, these practices are powerful tools to unleash our inner power and master our mindset for a fulfilling and prosperous life.

Summary

Feel free to write down any after-reading insights and thoughts

After reading this, I feel right now...

Chapter 7: Overcoming Obstacles and Maintaining a Resilient Mindset

Identifying and Overcoming Self-Doubt and Limiting Beliefs

Introduction:

Self-doubt and limiting beliefs can be powerful obstacles to personal transformation and success. They can hold us back from reaching our full potential and hinder our ability to achieve our goals. This subchapter will explore identifying and overcoming self-doubt and limiting beliefs to unleash your inner power and master your mindset for personal transformation.

Understanding Self-Doubt and Limiting Beliefs:

Self-doubt is that nagging voice that tells us we're not good, smart, or capable enough. It stems from a lack of confidence in our abilities and often leads to procrastination, fear of failure, and a negative self-image. Limiting beliefs, on the other hand, are deeply ingrained assumptions or thought patterns that restrict our potential. They can be related to money, relationships, success, or any area of life where we feel stuck.

Identifying Self-Doubt and Limiting Beliefs:

To overcome self-doubt and limiting beliefs, it is crucial to identify them first. Start by paying attention to your thoughts and emotions. What recurring negative thoughts do you have about yourself or your abilities? What beliefs do you hold about success, money, or relationships? Write them down and be honest with yourself. These insights will help you uncover the root causes of your self-doubt and limiting beliefs.

Challenging and Replacing Limiting Beliefs:

Once you've identified your limiting beliefs, it's time to challenge them. Ask yourself whether these beliefs are based on facts or simply assumptions. Look for evidence that contradicts your limiting beliefs and find counterexamples of people who have achieved what you desire.

Replace your old beliefs with new, empowering ones that support your personal growth and success. Repeat positive afirmations daily to reinforce these new beliefs.

Building Self-Confidence:

Self-doubt often stems from a lack of self-confidence. To build self-confidence, set small, achievable goals and celebrate your successes. Surround yourself with positive and supportive individuals who believe in your abilities. Practice self-care and invest time in activities that make you feel good about yourself. The more you build your self-confidence, the easier it becomes to overcome self-doubt and limiting beliefs.

Conclusion:

Identifying and overcoming self-doubt and limiting beliefs is crucial for personal transformation and success. By understanding the nature of self-doubt and limiting beliefs and actively challenging and replacing them with empowering beliefs, you can unleash your inner power and master your mindset. Building self-confidence and surrounding yourself with positivity will further support your journey towards personal transformation and success.

Remember, you can overcome self-doubt and limiting beliefs. You deserve to live a life of abundance, purpose, and fulfillment. Start today by taking the necessary steps to identify and overcome your self-doubt and limiting beliefs, and watch as you unlock your true potential for personal and professional success.

Strategies for Overcoming Procrastination and Taking Action

Introduction:

In our journey towards personal transformation, procrastination is one of the biggest obstacles we often face. We all have experienced moments when we know exactly what needs to be done, but we still find ourselves putting it off. However, overcoming procrastination is essential for mastering our mindset and achieving personal transformation. In this subchapter, we will explore practical strategies that can help individuals in various niches, such as Master Your Mindset, Mindset Mastery for Entrepreneurs, and Mindset for Financial Abundance, to overcome procrastination and take action toward their goals.

Set Clear and Specific Goals:

One of the first steps towards overcoming procrastination is setting clear and specific goals. By defining what you want to achieve, you create a clear path for action. Break down your goals into smaller, manageable tasks, and set deadlines for each task. This will give you a sense of urgency and increase your motivation to act.

Prioritize and Focus:

To avoid feeling overwhelmed and putting things off, it is crucial to prioritize your tasks. Identify the most critical and urgent tasks and focus on them first. You can avoid distractions and increase your productivity by focusing on one task at a time. Use time management techniques like the Pomodoro Technique to maintain focus and break tasks into manageable time intervals.

Overcome Procrastination Triggers:

Identify the triggers that lead to procrastination and find ways to overcome them. It could be fear of failure, perfectionism, or lack of motivation. Challenge negative thoughts and replace them with positive afirmations. Visualize the successful completion of your tasks and remind yourself of the benefits and rewards that await you.

Overcome Procrastination Triggers:

Identify the triggers that lead to procrastination and find ways to overcome them. It could be fear of failure, perfectionism, or lack of motivation. Challenge negative thoughts and replace them with positive afirmations. Visualize the successful completion of your tasks and remind yourself of the benefits and rewards that await you.

Create Accountability:

Accountability is a powerful tool for overcoming procrastination. Share your goals and progress with a trusted friend, mentor, or coach. They can provide support and encouragement and hold you accountable for your actions. Consider joining a mastermind group or finding an accountability partner to keep you motivated and on track.

Break Tasks into Smaller Steps:

Large tasks can be overwhelming and lead to procrastination. Break them down into smaller, more manageable steps. This will not only make the task seem less daunting but also give you a sense of accomplishment as you complete each step. Celebrate these small wins to boost your motivation and momentum.

Conclusion:

Overcoming procrastination is critical to personal transformation and achieving success in various niches, including Master Your Mindset, Mindset Mastery for Entrepreneurs, and Mindset for Financial Abundance. By setting clear goals, prioritizing tasks, overcoming procrastination triggers, creating accountability, and breaking tasks into smaller steps, individuals can unleash their inner power, master their mindset, and take consistent action toward their goals. Remember, the journey towards personal transformation begins with a single step, so start taking action today and unlock your full potential for success and abundance.

Dealing with Criticism and Rejection with a Resilient Mindset

In our journey towards personal transformation, we often encounter criticism and rejection. Whether it's in our personal relationships, professional endeavors, or financial pursuits, these experiences can be incredibly challenging and disheartening. However, how we respond to these setbacks genuinely defines our ability to unleash our inner power and master our mindset.

Developing a resilient mindset is crucial when faced with criticism and rejection. Our ability to bounce back from these obstacles determines our growth and success. So, how can we cultivate this resilient mindset?

Firstly, it's important to remember that criticism does not reflect our worth or abilities. Often, it is simply someone else's opinion or perspective. Instead of internalizing it as a personal attack, view it as an opportunity for growth and self-improvement. Ask yourself, "What can I learn from this criticism? How can I use it to become a better version of myself?"

Secondly, rejection is not a permanent state. It is merely a temporary setback on our journey toward success. Instead of dwelling on the rejection, focus on the lessons learned and the potential opportunities. Remember, every successful individual has faced rejection at some point. It is how they responded to it that propelled them forward.

Additionally, surrounding ourselves with a supportive network of individuals who uplift and encourage us is crucial in dealing with criticism and rejection. Seek mentors, coaches, and like-minded individuals who understand your challenges. They can provide guidance and support and help you maintain a positive mindset during dificult times.

Lastly, practice self-compassion and self-care. We must prioritize our well-being and nurture ourselves emotionally, physically, and mentally. Engage in activities that bring you joy and help you maintain a positive mindset. Take time for self-reflection and celebrate your achievements, no matter how small they may seem.

In conclusion, dealing with criticism and rejection requires a resilient mindset. By viewing these experiences as opportunities for growth, surrounding ourselves with a supportive network, and practicing self-compassion, we can overcome these obstacles and unleash our inner power. Remember, setbacks are an integral part of the journey towards personal transformation. Embrace, learn from, and use them to propel yourself towards success.

Cultivating Perseverance and Grit in the Face of Challenges

Challenges are inevitable in the journey towards personal transformation. They test our resilience, determination, and ability to persevere. It is during these challenging times that our mindset becomes crucial in shaping our outcomes. In this subchapter, we will explore the importance of cultivating perseverance and grit and how it can lead to personal growth and success in various areas of life.

For individuals embarking on their personal transformation journey, it is essential to understand that setbacks and obstacles are not roadblocks but growth opportunities. Developing perseverance and grit allows us to navigate these challenges with resilience and determination.

Perseverance and grit are the cornerstones of success in mastering one's mindset. They enable individuals to overcome self-doubt, push through limiting beliefs, and focus on their goals. By cultivating these qualities, individuals can develop a growth mindset that embraces challenges as opportunities for learning and growth.

Entrepreneurs, in particular, can benefit significantly from developing perseverance and grit. The entrepreneurial journey is filled with ups and downs and common setbacks. However, those who can persevere and maintain their focus even in the face of adversity are more likely to achieve business success. This subchapter will provide practical strategies and mindset shifts that entrepreneurs can implement to cultivate perseverance and grit for unlocking their potential and achieving their business goals.

Furthermore, developing a wealth mindset is essential for financial abundance and prosperity. Individuals with perseverance and grit are more likely to overcome economic challenges and setbacks. They can bounce back from failures, learn from them, and continue progressing toward their financial goals. This subchapter will delve into the mindset shifts and strategies necessary for cultivating perseverance and grit in pursuing economic freedom and abundance.

In conclusion, cultivating perseverance and grit is crucial for personal transformation and success. This subchapter will explore strategies and mindset shifts necessary to develop these qualities. Whether you are seeking to master your mindset, unlock your potential as an entrepreneur, or cultivate a wealth mindset, the ability to persevere and maintain grit will be instrumental in overcoming challenges and achieving your desired outcomes. Embrace the power of perseverance and grit, and unlock your inner power for personal transformation and success.

Summary

Feel free to write down any after-reading insights and thoughts

After reading this, I feel right now...

Chapter 8: Building a Supportive Mindset for Personal Transformation

Surrounding Yourself with Positive Influences and Mentors

We are greatly influenced by the people we surround ourselves with. Our environment plays a crucial role in shaping our mindset and determining our success. Suppose we want to unleash our inner power and transform our lives. In that case, we must surround ourselves with positive influences and mentors who can guide us toward personal transformation.

Positive influences can come in various forms, such as friends, family members, colleagues, or virtual mentors. These individuals radiate positivity, inspire us with their success stories, and uplift our spirits in adversity. By surrounding ourselves with positive influences, we can cultivate a mindset of optimism, resilience, and growth.

Mentors, on the other hand, are individuals who have already achieved what we aspire to accomplish. They are experts in their respective fields and possess a wealth of knowledge and experience. Having a mentor can provide us with valuable insights, advice, and guidance, accelerating our personal transformation journey. They can help us navigate challenges, avoid pitfalls, and unlock our potential.

For individuals seeking personal transformation, mastering their mindset is crucial. The subchapter "Surrounding Yourself with Positive Influences and Mentors" addresses the significance of surrounding oneself with positive influences and mentors in various niches.

For those looking to master their mindset for personal transformation, surrounding themselves with like- minded individuals who are also on a journey of self-improvement can be incredibly beneficial. Sharing experiences, challenges, and successes can create a supportive network that fosters personal growth and development.

Entrepreneurs, too, can significantly benefit from surrounding themselves with positive influences and mentors who have achieved business success. These mentors can guide strategic decision-making, overcoming obstacles, and building a resilient mindset necessary for entrepreneurial endeavors.

Individuals seeking financial abundance and freedom can cultivate a wealth mindset by surrounding themselves with mentors who have achieved financial success. These mentors can share insights on wealth creation, investment strategies, and cultivating a positive relationship with money.

In conclusion, surrounding ourselves with positive influences and mentors is a transformative step towards unleashing our inner power. By immersing ourselves in an environment that fosters growth, resilience, and success, we can master our mindset and achieve personal transformation. Whether through like-minded communities, business mentors, or financial experts, seeking guidance and support from positive influences is essential to our journey toward personal transformation.

The Power of Accountability and Support Systems

In our journey towards personal transformation, one of the most powerful tools we can utilize is the concept of accountability and having a solid support system. It is often said that we are the average of the five people we spend the most time with, and this couldn't be more true. Surrounding ourselves with driven, ambitious individuals who share similar goals can significantly impact our mindset and propel us toward success.

Accountability serves as a compass that keeps us on track toward our goals. When we have someone to hold us accountable for our actions, it becomes harder to make excuses or stray from the path we have set for ourselves. This external source of accountability can come in various forms, such as a mentor, a coach, or even a trusted friend. Regularly checking in with someone who understands our objectives and desires makes us more likely to stay focused and committed.

A support system can also provide encouragement and motivation to push through challenges. Transformation is not always an easy process, and there will be moments when we doubt ourselves or face obstacles that seem insurmountable. However, when we have a network of like-minded individuals who believe in us and our abilities, we gain the strength to persevere. They can offer guidance, share their experiences, and provide emotional support to keep us going.

Having a solid support system becomes even more crucial for those seeking personal transformation in entrepreneurship. The entrepreneurial journey is filled with uncertainties, risks, and setbacks. It is during these times that having a network of fellow entrepreneurs who have faced similar challenges can make all the difference. They can offer advice, share strategies, and serve as a sounding board for ideas. With their support, we can navigate the complexities of business and unlock our full potential for success.

Similarly, for individuals seeking financial abundance, cultivating a wealth mindset and building a support system for individuals who have achieved financial freedom is vital. By surrounding ourselves with individuals focused on prosperity and abundance, we can adopt their beliefs and habits that lead to economic success. We can learn from their experiences, gain valuable insights, and develop the necessary mindset to attract wealth into our lives.

In conclusion, the power of accountability and support systems cannot be overstated. To unleash our inner power and master our mindset for personal transformation, we must surround ourselves with individuals who inspire and challenge us.

Whether in entrepreneurship, personal growth, or financial abundance, having a strong support system and being held accountable for our actions will accelerate our progress toward our goals. Together, we can achieve greatness and create the life we desire.

Creating a Personal Success Network for Mutual Growth

In today's fast-paced and highly competitive world, personal success is no longer just about individual effort. It is increasingly becoming a collective journey that requires the support and collaboration of like-minded individuals. By creating a personal success network, you can tap into the power of mutual growth and unlock your full potential for personal transformation.

The concept of a personal success network is rooted in the belief that surrounding yourself with individuals who share similar goals and aspirations can significantly enhance your chances of success. This network can comprise mentors, peers, colleagues, and even friends dedicated to personal growth and self-improvement.

One key aspect of building a personal success network is finding individuals who have already mastered the mindset required for personal transformation. These individuals can serve as mentors and role models, guiding you toward unleashing your inner power. Their experiences and wisdom can provide valuable insights and help you avoid common pitfalls.

For entrepreneurs seeking to achieve business success, a personal success network can be a game- changer. By connecting with other like-minded entrepreneurs who have already mastered the art of mindset mastery, you can gain access to a wealth of knowledge and resources. This network can provide valuable feedback, support, and potential business partnerships, fueling your entrepreneurial journey toward success.

Similarly, cultivating a personal success network is crucial for those seeking financial abundance and freedom.

Surrounding yourself with individuals who have already achieved financial success can help you develop a wealth mindset and gain insights into the strategies and habits that lead to prosperity. Their guidance and support can be invaluable as you achieve your financial goals.

Creating a personal success network is not just about finding individuals who can help you; it is also about offering your support and expertise to others. By contributing to the growth and success of others, you create a reciprocal relationship that fosters mutual growth. This sense of community and collaboration can be incredibly empowering and provide a strong foundation for personal transformation.

In conclusion, creating a personal success network is essential for individuals seeking personal transformation in various niches, such as mastering mindset, entrepreneurship, and financial abundance. By surrounding yourself with like-minded individuals, you can tap into a wealth of knowledge, support, and collaboration, accelerating your journey toward personal success. Remember, success is no longer a solitary endeavor; it is a collective effort fueled by the power of an individual success network.

Paying It Forward: Sharing Your Mindset Transformation with Others

One of the most potent aspects of personal transformation is the ability to inspire and uplift others through your journey. As you master your mindset, it's essential to recognize the impact you can have on those around you. By sharing your transformation, you solidify your growth and become a catalyst for positive change in the lives of others.

In the book "Unleashing Your Inner Power: Mastering Your Mindset for Personal Transformation," we understand the importance of paying it forward and its profound effect on individuals seeking personal growth. Whether you are striving to master your mindset for personal transformation, unlock your potential for business success as an entrepreneur, or cultivate a wealth mindset for financial abundance, sharing your journey can be a game-changer.

When you share your mindset transformation, you provide others with a blueprint for their success. You exemplify what is possible when one commits to growth and self-improvement. By openly discussing the obstacles you've overcome and the strategies you've employed, you empower others to take action and embark on their transformative journey.

Moreover, sharing your transformation can be a source of motivation and inspiration for entrepreneurs. As you navigate the challenges and triumphs of building a successful business, your mindset becomes crucial in achieving your goals. By sharing your mindset mastery with fellow entrepreneurs, you can help them unlock their potential and overcome limiting beliefs that may hold them back. This empowers them to take decisive action and propel their businesses to new heights.

Cultivating a wealth mindset is paramount for those seeking financial abundance. By sharing your journey towards financial freedom, you provide others with the tools and mindset shifts necessary to attract prosperity into their lives. As you demonstrate the power of abundance thinking and the importance of taking calculated risks, you inspire individuals to break free from scarcity mindsets and embrace an attitude of abundance.

In conclusion, sharing your mindset transformation is a powerful way to pay it forward and positively impact the lives of others. Whether focused on personal transformation, entrepreneurial success, or financial abundance, your journey is a blueprint for others to follow. By openly discussing the strategies, mindset shifts, and obstacles you've faced, you empower individuals to take action and transform their lives. Remember, your transformation has the potential to inspire and uplift others, creating a ripple effect of positivity and growth within your community.

Summary

Feel free to write down any after-reading insights and thoughts

After reading this, I feel right now...

____

____

____

____

____

____

Chapter 9: Sustaining Your Mindset for Life-long Personal Transformation

The Importance of Continuous Learning and Growth

In today's fast-paced and ever-evolving world, the importance of continuous learning and growth cannot be overstated. This subchapter delves into the significance of embracing a mindset that values personal development and explores its relevance to three specific niches: Master Your Mindset, Mindset Mastery for Entrepreneurs, and Mindset for Financial Abundance.

Master Your Mindset: The Definitive Blueprint for Personal Transformation

Mastering your mindset is the cornerstone of personal transformation. It involves developing a deep understanding of your thoughts, beliefs, and behavior patterns and actively working to reshape them for positive change. Continuous learning is crucial in this process, as it allows you to expand your knowledge, challenge limiting beliefs, and develop new strategies for personal growth. By investing time and effort into learning about mindset techniques, psychological principles, and self-improvement strategies, you gain the tools necessary to unleash your inner power and transform your life.

Mindset Mastery for Entrepreneurs: Unlocking Your Potential to Achieve Business Success

For entrepreneurs, continuous learning and growth are essential for achieving business success. As an entrepreneur, you face unique challenges and responsibilities. By continuously expanding your knowledge and skills, you stay ahead of the curve, adapt to changing market trends, and make informed decisions that drive your business forward.

Learning from industry experts, attending seminars, and networking with like-minded individuals provide invaluable opportunities to gain insights, exchange ideas, and learn from others' experiences. Embracing a growth mindset allows you to persevere through obstacles, learn from failures, and ultimately unlock your potential as an entrepreneur.

Mindset for Financial Abundance: Cultivating a Wealth Mindset for Prosperity and Financial Freedom

Cultivating a wealth mindset is the key to attaining financial abundance and freedom. Continuous learning about money management, investment strategies, and financial planning empowers individuals to make informed decisions and take control of their financial future. By studying successful individuals and learning from their wealth-building strategy, you can adopt a mindset that attracts prosperity and abundance. Continuous growth in financial literacy allows you to identify opportunities, make sound investments, and build wealth over time.

In conclusion, continuous learning and growth are vital for personal transformation, entrepreneurial success, and financial abundance. By embracing a mindset that values personal development, individuals can unlock their inner power, achieve business success, and cultivate a wealth mindset. Through continuous learning, individuals can expand their knowledge, challenge their beliefs, and develop strategies that propel them towards their goals. So, take the initiative today and embark on a continuous learning and growth journey, for it is the pathway to unleashing your inner power and living a life of fulfillment and abundance.

Strategies for Maintaining Motivation and Momentum

Maintaining motivation and momentum is one of the most significant challenges we face in our journey toward personal transformation. Whether we seek to master our mindset, achieve business success as entrepreneurs, or cultivate a wealth mindset for financial abundance, our ability to stay motivated and keep moving forward is crucial.

This subchapter will explore practical strategies to help individuals in various niches sustain their motivation and maintain momentum on their path to personal growth and success.

Firstly, it is essential to set clear and specific goals. It becomes challenging to stay motivated and focused without a clear destination in mind. Clearly define your objectives, breaking them down into smaller, achievable steps. This way, you can track your progress and celebrate each milestone, fueling your motivation.

Moreover, surround yourself with positive and like-minded individuals. Join communities or networks that align with your niche, such as Master Your Mindset or Mindset Mastery for Entrepreneurs. Interacting with individuals who share similar goals and challenges can provide valuable support, encouragement, and accountability. Their energy and enthusiasm will help you stay motivated, especially during dificult times.

Another powerful strategy is to cultivate a growth mindset. Embrace challenges as opportunities for growth and learning. Understand that setbacks and failures are an inevitable part of personal transformation. Instead of being discouraged, view them as valuable lessons and stepping stones towards success. Adopting a growth mindset allows you to maintain motivation by focusing on progress rather than perfection.

Additionally, regularly review your progress and celebrate your achievements. Take time to reflect on how far you've come and acknowledge the effort and dedication you've invested. Celebrating small victories boosts your motivation and reinforces positive habits and behaviors.

Lastly, incorporate self-care practices into your routine. Taking care of your physical, mental, and emotional well-being is vital for maintaining motivation and momentum. Prioritize activities that recharge and rejuvenate you, whether exercise, meditation, leisure time in nature, or hobbies. When you prioritize self-care, you enhance your overall energy levels and increase your capacity for sustained motivation.

In conclusion, maintaining motivation and momentum is a continuous process that requires conscious effort. By setting clear goals, surrounding themselves with positive influences, cultivating a growth mindset, celebrating achievements, and prioritizing self-care, individuals in various niches can sustain their motivation and maintain momentum on their journey toward personal transformation and success. Remember, motivation is not a one-time event but a constant practice that fuels your inner power and enables you to unleash your fullest potential.

Overcoming Setbacks and Bouncing Back Stronger

Life is full of challenges, and setbacks are inevitable in our journey toward personal transformation. Whether you are seeking to master your mindset, achieve business success, or cultivate financial abundance, setbacks will test your resilience and determination. However, how you respond to these setbacks genuinely defines your ability to bounce back more vital than ever before.

In the face of adversity, it is essential to recognize that setbacks are not failures but growth opportunities. They are valuable lessons that propel you toward personal and professional success. By embracing setbacks and viewing them as stepping stones rather than stumbling blocks, you can unleash your inner power and transform your mindset.

Adopting a growth mindset is one of the first steps in overcoming setbacks. This mindset allows you to see challenges as opportunities for learning and improvement. Instead of dwelling on past failures, focus on what you can do differently and how you can use setbacks as catalysts for growth. Remember, setbacks are not permanent roadblocks but temporary hurdles that can be overcome with the right mindset.

Additionally, it is crucial to cultivate resilience. Resilience is the ability to bounce back from adversity and maintain a positive outlook despite setbacks. It involves developing a solid mental and emotional fortitude to persevere in facing challenges. By practicing resilience, you can confidently navigate through setbacks and emerge stronger on the other side.

Moreover, setbacks provide an opportunity for self-reflection and self-discovery. Take the time to analyze what went wrong and identify areas for improvement. This introspection will help you uncover your strengths and weaknesses, enabling you to make necessary adjustments for future success. Remember, setbacks are not setbacks if they lead to self-awareness and personal growth.

In pursuing personal transformation, setbacks are not to be feared but embraced. They are the catalysts that propel you towards your goals and aspirations. By developing a growth mindset, cultivating resilience, and engaging in self-reflection, you can overcome setbacks and bounce back more vital than ever before.

So, the next time you encounter a setback on your journey towards mastering your mindset, achieving business success, or cultivating financial abundance, remember that setbacks are not permanent roadblocks but stepping stones toward personal transformation. Embrace the challenges, learn from them, and let them fuel your determination to bounce back, which is more vital than ever. Unleash your inner power and transform your mindset for a future filled with success, abundance, and personal growth.

Embracing Your Inner Power: A Lifetime Commitment to Personal Transformation

In the journey of personal transformation, the most potent tool lies within you - your inner power. It is the driving force that fuels your passion, ignites your dreams, and propels you towards success. This subchapter, titled "Embracing Your Inner Power: A Lifetime Commitment to Personal Transformation," aims to guide and inspire individuals across various niches, including "Master Your Mindset: The Definitive Blueprint for Personal Transformation," "Mindset Mastery for Entrepreneurs: Unlocking Your Potential to Achieve Business Success," and "Mindset for Financial Abundance: Cultivating a Wealth Mindset for Prosperity and Financial Freedom."

Understanding and embracing your inner power is not a one-time endeavor but a lifelong commitment. It requires consistent effort, self-reflection, and a willingness to challenge and overcome limiting beliefs. Acknowledging your inner power can shape your reality and create your desired life.

To embark on this transformative journey, it is crucial to develop a growth mindset. This mindset allows you to view challenges as opportunities for growth rather than obstacles to your progress. Adopting a growth mindset cultivates resilience, perseverance, and a willingness to learn from successes and failures.

Furthermore, self-awareness plays a vital role in harnessing one's inner power. Understanding one's strengths, weaknesses, values, and aspirations can align one's actions with one's authentic self. This self-awareness empowers one to make conscious choices and take intentional steps towards personal transformation.

Embracing your inner power also involves developing a positive mindset. By focusing on gratitude, afirmations, and positive self-talk, you can rewire your brain for optimism and resilience. This mindset shift allows you to overcome self-doubt, conquer fear, and unlock your full potential.

Additionally, cultivating a growth-oriented support system is crucial for personal transformation. Surrounding yourself with like-minded individuals who share your commitment to growth and support your aspirations can provide invaluable guidance, encouragement, and accountability.

Ultimately, embracing your inner power is a lifelong journey of self-discovery, growth, and transformation. Committing to this path can unleash your true potential and create a life of fulfillment, success, and abundance.

Whether you seek personal transformation, entrepreneurial success, or financial abundance, the key lies in harnessing your inner power. Embrace this lifelong commitment to unleashing your inner power and embark on a transformative journey toward achieving your dreams and creating the life you deserve.

www.ingramcontent.com/pod-product-compliance
Lightning Source LLC
LaVergne TN
LVHW052032170826
845678LV00020B/3222

* 9 7 8 3 2 9 7 1 8 3 1 2 0 *